SEASONAL WEATHER

SUMMER
WEATHER

John Mason

Wayland

Seasonal Weather

Spring Weather
Summer Weather
Autumn Weather
Winter Weather

Cover: Sunbathers enjoy hot summer weather on the beaches of the Cote d'Azur near Nice in France.

Opposite: A major lightning storm lights up the sky on a summer evening in California, USA.

Edited by Sarah Doughty
Series designed by Derek Lee

First published in 1990 by
Wayland (Publishers) Ltd
61, Western Road, Hove
East Sussex, BN3 1JD, England

British Library Cataloguing in Publication Data
Mason, John
  Summer weather
  1. Climate
  I. Title II. Series
  551.6

  ISBN 1–85210–942–4

Typeset by Rachel Gibbs, Wayland
Printed and bound by Casterman S.A., Belgium

CONTENTS

The summer season

Most of us have enjoyed hot summer weather when the Sun shines all day from a clear, blue sky. But some parts of the world have no real summer at all. At the **poles**, there is thick snow and ice all year, even in summer when the Sun shines for twenty-four hours a day. The short, warm **Arctic** summer lasts just six weeks, but in the **Antarctic** it is very cold all the time.

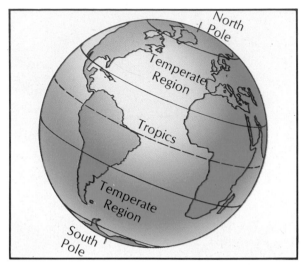
▲ **A diagram showing the main zones of climate on Earth.**

People enjoying the summer Sun at Takapuna, Auckland, New Zealand.

Tropical Barbados with its clear blue sky, palm trees and white sandy beaches in the summer.

In the **tropics**, the length of day and night varies little during the year and it is always warm. Close to the **Equator** where the great rainforests grow, it is very hot and there is heavy rain all year round. Elsewhere in the tropics, there are really only two main seasons. One season is extremely hot and usually very wet, the other is dry and a little cooler.

Between the tropics and the poles are mild **temperate regions**, where the length of day and night varies during the year. It stays light until late evening in summer. Here there are clear changes in the weather from one season to another. This is a never-ending cycle – spring, summer, autumn and winter, but it takes many weeks for one season to change to the next.

Near the poles it is always cold, even in summer, and icebergs remain all year.

Why seasons happen

The Earth travels around the Sun, going round it once every year. The Earth also spins on its **axis**. This axis is not upright but leans over at an angle of 23.5°. It is this tilt which causes the seasons. When the northern **hemisphere** leans towards the Sun the temperate lands of the north enjoy warm summer weather. Meanwhile the southern hemisphere which is tilted away has its winter.

▲ **The Sun lights up half of the Earth at a time creating day and night.**

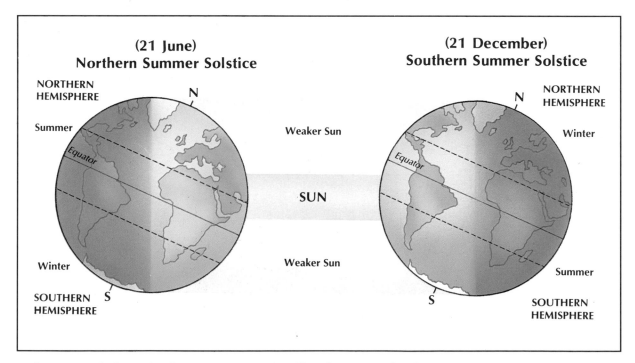

When each hemisphere in turn is tilted towards the Sun, it is summer in that half of the world and winter in the other.

The Sun rising over the Heel Stone in midsummer at Stonehenge, Britain.

Six months later the positions are reversed. The southern hemisphere then leans towards the Sun and has its summer. At the same time, the northern hemisphere is tilted away and it is winter.

As the northern hemisphere tilts towards the Sun, days become longer in northern temperate lands. The longest day falls on 21 June. This is the Summer Solstice (or Midsummer Day) and comes near the beginning of summer, not in the middle.

In the temperate regions of the southern hemisphere, summer occurs in December, January and February. The hottest weather comes in late January or February, long after the Summer Solstice has occurred, on 21 December.

Northern Hemisphere			
Autumn	Winter	Spring	Summer
September	December	March	June
October	January	April	July
November	February	May	August
Spring	Summer	Autumn	Winter
Southern Hemisphere			

Sunshine and temperature

All life on Earth needs the heat and light of the Sun. The sunlight filters through the atmosphere and warms the land and sea. Because the Earth's surface is curved, the Sun's rays heat the Earth unevenly.

In the tropics, the Sun is always nearly overhead at midday. Here, sunlight has the shortest distance to travel through the atmosphere and it is always hot. Further away from the Equator, the Sun's rays are weakened, because they travel further through the atmosphere to reach the ground. They pass through the thickest layer of atmosphere to reach the poles. This makes the Sun's rays weakest in the polar regions, so it is never very warm.

In summer, the Sun rises higher in the sky at midday than in winter, so the days are longer. The Sun's rays also strike the ground at a steeper angle and are spread over a smaller area, so their heating effect is greater.

The 'midnight Sun' never sets in the summer over northern Norway.

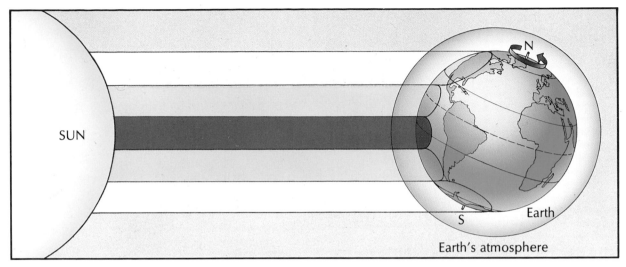

▲ The Sun's rays gradually become weaker further from the Equator.

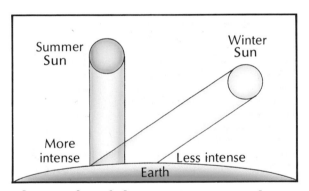

The angle of the Sun's rays makes it warmer in summer than winter.

When the Sun is high in the sky, its rays have a shorter path through the atmosphere to the ground, so less heat is lost than when it is low down. The strength of the Sun's rays and the longer days make summer warmer than winter.

Highest Recorded Temperatures

AFRICA
Al-Azizyah, Libya   58°C/136.4°F

AMERICA
Death Valley,
California   57°C/134.6°F

ASIA
Tirat Tsvi, Israel   54°C/129.2°F

AUSTRALIA
Cloncurry,
Queensland   53°C/127.4°F

EUROPE
Seville, Spain   50°C/122°F

ANTARCTICA
Esperanza, Palmer   14°C/57.2°F

9

Air pressure and winds

When air is warmed by the Sun's rays, it expands becoming thinner and lighter. This warm air rises and pushes down less on the ground, so the **air pressure** is low. Cold air is heavier, and it sinks, pushing down on the ground. This forms an area of high pressure. Winds are caused by the movement of air from areas of high pressure towards areas where the pressure is lower.

Over the poles, the cold air sinks causing permanent areas of high pressure. This sinking, cool air spreads out towards the temperate regions. Near the Equator, the air is warm and a band of low pressure is always present. This warm air rises, spreading north and south. This movement creates further bands of high and low pressure between the Equator and the poles. These produce the world's main winds.

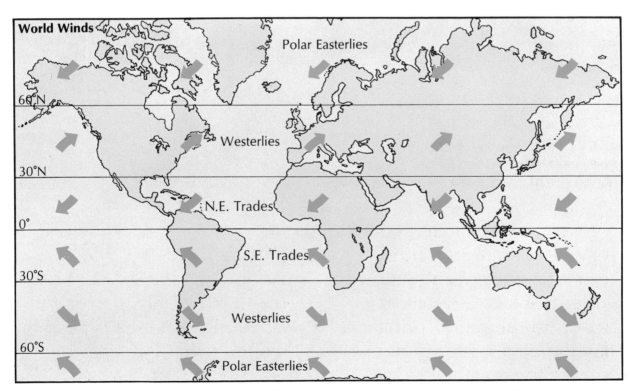

Diagram showing where the main surface winds blow on Earth.

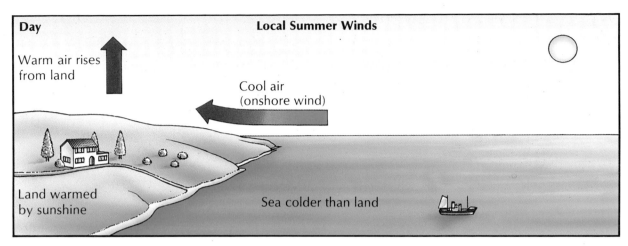

▲ **During the day, a breeze can blow from the sea towards the land.**

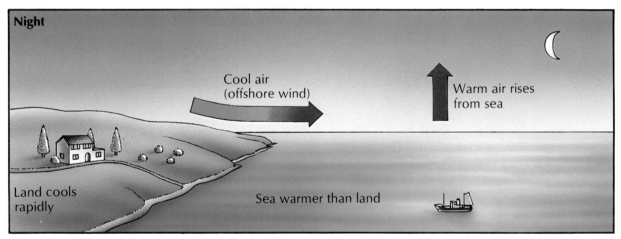

▲ **At night, a breeze can blow from the land towards the sea.**

Near the coast in temperate regions and parts of the tropics, a daily, local wind called a sea breeze often occurs in summer. During the day the land heats up quickly, but it also cools quickly at night. The sea heats up slowly, but holds its heat for longer. In the daytime, the land is warmer than the sea, and sea breezes blow inland from the sea. At night the sea is warmer than the land, and land breezes blow from land out to sea.

Rain and hail

Wherever water is warmed by the Sun's rays, some of it evaporates and is held in the air as invisible water vapour. Warm air can hold more water vapour than cold air. As warm, moist air rises into the atmosphere where it is colder, it becomes **saturated**. It cannot then absorb any more water vapour.

▲ **Sudden showers can fall at any time, even when the Sun shines.**

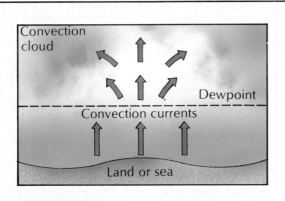

◄ Clouds develop when the ground or sea is heated, causing warm air to rise and cool. Thunderclouds often form, and heavy rain falls.

Most sea winds rise when they cross over ► mountain ranges. Cooling leads to clouds and rain on coastal slopes.

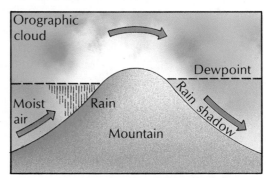

◄ Clouds and rain occur when warm air rises over cold air along a front, and cools.

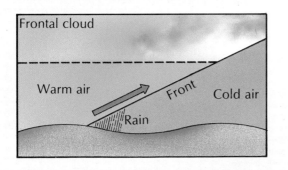

The formation of the three main types of rainfall.

A heavy hailstorm has devastated a field of corn in Indiana, USA.

If this air is cooled below a certain temperature called the **dewpoint**, some of the water **condenses** out into tiny water droplets. These become visible as clouds. The droplets collide with others becoming larger and heavier, until they fall as rain.

Rain can be caused in three ways. When hot air laden with water vapour rises and cools, it condenses and falls as convection rain. As warm, moist air rises up over mountains or hills, the temperature drops and the water vapour condenses to fall as orographic rain. If a region of warm, moist air rises up over an area of cool air, clouds form along the **front** and rain occurs.

If raindrops are carried by rising air to the top of a cloud they may freeze, forming **hailstones**. Buffeted by strong winds, the hailstones rise and fall within the cloud gathering more layers of ice until they become so heavy that they fall to the ground.

The summer monsoon

In parts of the tropics, monsoon winds are common. Monsoons are winds that change direction with the season. They occur because of differences in land and sea temperatures at different times of the year. Monsoon winds blow from cool towards warmer regions; from sea towards the land in summer and from land towards the sea in winter.

In early summer, the air above the land rises as it is heated. This creates a region of low pressure. Air is sucked into this low pressure region causing a wind to blow. Over southern Asia, south-westerly monsoon winds tend to blow from June to October, continuing in the south until December.

The summer monsoon winds are warm and moist.

Monsoon rain clouds gather off the coast of Sri Lanka.

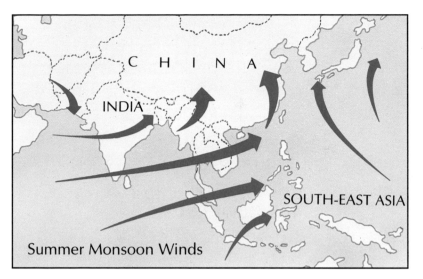

◀ **The direction of monsoon winds over parts of Asia in summer.**

▼ **Severe flooding in Calcutta, India, caused by monsoon rains.**

They blow across the Indian Ocean towards southern Asia, carrying moisture evaporated from the sea. When they reach land these winds bring steamy and uncomfortable conditions, violent thunderstorms and torrential rain to coastal and upland areas.

Inland areas have heavy rain in some years, but in others there is little or none. Monsoon rains may cause severe flooding. People and animals drown and crops are destroyed. If the monsoon rains fail to arrive, **drought** causes starvation and death later in the year.

Thunder and lightning

In summer, thunderstorms occur when warm, moist air rises and cools. The water vapour within it condenses to form **cumulus** clouds, which billow upwards like huge mushrooms until they reach a height of between 10 km and 14 km. Here the cloud top flattens out into an anvil shape. Eventually several cumulus clouds combine into a towering cumulonimbus or thundercloud.

Thunderstorms always include lightning followed by its noisy companion – thunder. A lightning flash is a giant electrical **spark** between an electrically-charged thundercloud and the ground, or between two clouds. Lightning occurs when raindrops inside the thundercloud acquire a negative electrical **charge**, while icy hailstones acquire a positive charge. The positive

Thunderstorms

Every year more than 16 million thunderstorms occur on Earth. Torrential rain or hail accompanies thunderstorms.

A single storm can release 500 million litres of water.

◀ **Spectacular lightning flashes during a major summer thunderstorm.**

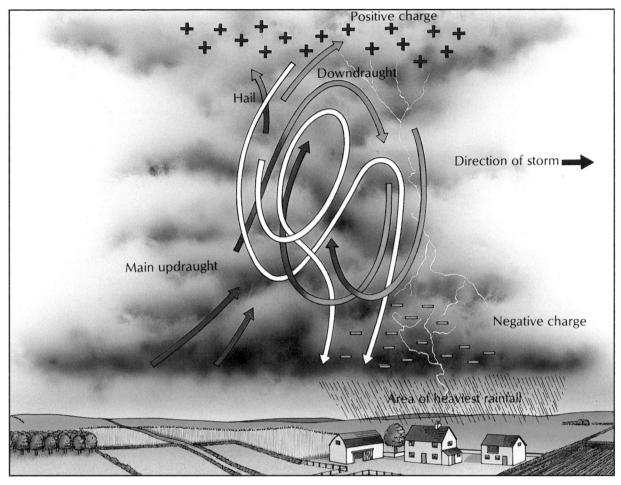

Positive charge

Downdraught

Hail

Direction of storm

Main updraught

Negative charge

Area of heaviest rainfall

A towering thundercloud showing the build-up of electrical charges.

charge usually collects at the top of the thundercloud while the lower parts contain negative charges.

A lightning flash often flickers and may last a second or two. Each flash may consist of a number of separate sparks, a fraction of a second apart. The lightning flash heats the air through which it passes to 30,000°C (over 54,000°F). This causes the surrounding air to expand very rapidly, creating a shock wave like the sonic boom of a supersonic aircraft. We hear it as the sound of thunder.

Tornadoes and waterspouts

In the summer a long line of thunderclouds may form. This is called a squall line. One or two of these thunderclouds may be very violent storms where the winds blow very strongly. These are called **supercell** thunderstorms.

Winds from outside the supercell are sucked into the centre. This causes the wind to speed up. It whirls around at speeds of up to 500 kph.

A whirling funnel called a **tornado** then forms from the bottom of the thundercloud. It grows steadily longer until it reaches the ground in an explosion of flying dirt.

The tornado funnel bumps along the ground sweeping up objects like a huge vacuum cleaner. In a large tornado, there may be three or more funnels which revolve around each other. Sometimes the

The twisting funnel of a tornado hits the ground in a flurry of flying dirt, near Oklahoma, USA.

◄ An aerial view of tornado damage in Kentucky, USA.

▼ A waterspout throws spray into the air as it moves across the sea.

funnels are like lengths of hosepipe. Others are snake-like and twitch like the tail of an angry cat.

Severe tornadoes rarely occur outside the USA but smaller short-lived ones are found elsewhere. Over the sea, **waterspouts** may form with wind speeds of up to 150 kph, although 80 kph is more normal. Waterspouts can cause damage if they cross land, but they never cause as much damage as tornadoes.

Summer in temperate regions

Summer weather varies a great deal in temperate lands. Northern and eastern Europe, New Zealand, eastern Australia, south-east USA and Turkey have warm summers and rain all year, even in summer. Parts of Europe often have cloudy skies in summer.

The Mediterranean countries, California, parts of Chile, the south-western tip of South Africa and parts of southern Australia all enjoy hot, dry, almost continuously sunny summers, although thunderstorms may occur.

In the northern USA and Canada, summers are dry but cooler. In central USA, a long way from the sea, summers are much hotter than coastal areas at the same **latitude**.

Close to the tropics, summer comes early and there is a long period of hot, dry weather. However, in northern Mexico it is much wetter in summer than winter. The northern part of Australia has

Flowering shrubs add a splash of colour to the tundra in Alaska.

Storm clouds gather over a French town on a summer afternoon.

tropical summer weather, but the southern part is temperate.

Near the Arctic, in Alaska, northern Canada, northern Scandinavia and Siberia, summer comes late. In the treeless **tundra**, the topsoil thaws, but just a few centimetres below the ground stays frozen. Mosses and flowers grow in the short, cool summers, when temperatures rise towards 10°C (50°F). However, there are often snowstorms and frosts which occur as late as the Summer Solstice.

Sunbathers enjoying the warm sunshine on a beach in summer.

Hot tropical lands

Along the Equator, a band of low pressure called the **Equatorial Trough** is always present. This region has a constant high temperature of 25-27°C (77-80.6°F) all year round. It also has very heavy rainfall, particularly in summer.

The Amazon River basin in South America has an average yearly rainfall of 2,000 mm or more. The African forests of the Zaire basin have less rain, but still get more than

Dense rainforest by the Amazon River near Tefe in Brazil.

The snow-capped Mount Kilimanjaro in Kenya, Africa's highest peak.

Zebra and giraffe roam the great grassland plains of the tropics.

1,300 mm a year. At the edge of the rainforests the trees thin out into woodlands. Beyond this lie great grassland plains with scattered trees. These regions have a marked dry season as well as the hot, wet season in summer.

If hot, dry weather continues for a long time, it can lead to a drought. In a drought rivers and water-holes dry up, plants wither and animals die.

Violent thunderstorms often occur after long, hot periods, bringing much-needed rain to bone-dry soil.

Altitude also affects the weather in the tropics. Mount Kilimanjaro in Kenya, which rises 5,895 m above sea-level, is Africa's highest peak. Although it is less than 400 km south of the Equator, it is snow-capped even in summer.

Summer in the deserts

Most of the world's hot deserts are found between latitudes 20-40° north and south of the Equator. Here, within bands of high pressure air, the Sun is always hot and little rain ever falls. Deserts usually have less than 250 mm of rain per year. Parts of the Atacama Desert in northern Chile have had no rain for 400 years. Most deserts have unreliable rainfall. The rains may come early or late or not at all in the three-month rainy season, and brief, violent storms sometimes cause flooding.

▲ Camels at a water-hole in the cold desert region of Mongolia.

Sand dunes and wild grasses in the north African desert of Morocco.

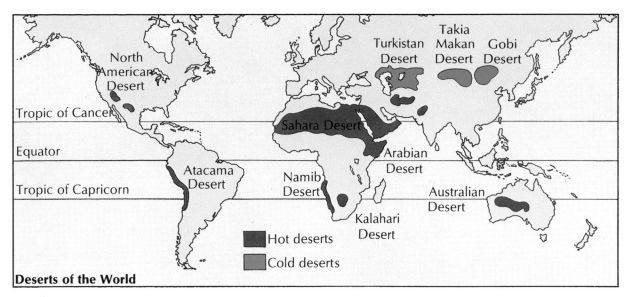

A map showing the world's major hot and cold deserts.

Under cloudless skies deserts become very hot during the day. At Aswan, Egypt, in the eastern Sahara Desert region, the highest temperature in the shade is around 30°C (86°F). In direct sunlight, the summer temperature has reached 87°C (189°F) in the eastern Sahara Desert, which has an average of more than ten hours of sunshine every day.

There are also cold, mid-latitude deserts in Asia. Cold deserts have cooler summers than hot deserts and cold winters. In the Gobi Desert in the heart of the Asian continent, the temperature in the hottest month only reaches about 15°C (59°F), slightly warmer than the coldest month at Aswan.

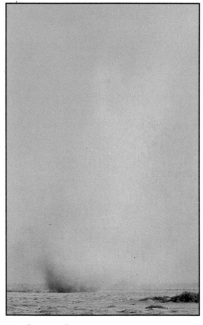

In hot deserts whirlwinds called dust devils often occur.

Global warming

The world is getting hotter. Over the past hundred years, the average global temperature has risen by 0.5°C (0.9°F). At the same time rainfall has increased in middle and high latitudes, but droughts have become more common in the tropics. Most scientists believe these changes are due to global warming, also called the 'greenhouse effect'.

▲ **Giant chimneys of a power station belch gases into the sky.**

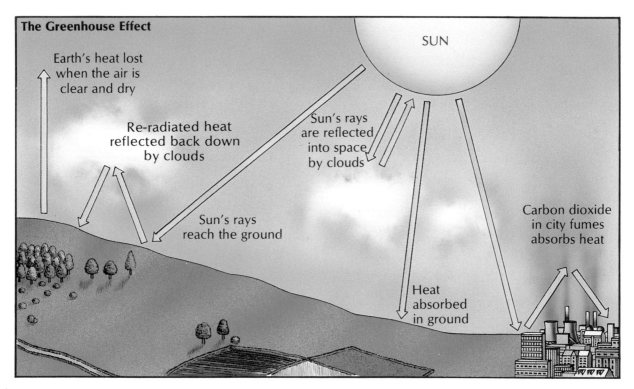

Some of the Sun's heat is not able to escape from the Earth's surface because certain gases in the air absorb or reflect it.

Every second 22 hectares of rainforest is destroyed somewhere.

Global warming is caused by the build-up in the atmosphere of **carbon dioxide** and other gases that trap heat which would otherwise be radiated out into space. These gases are building up rapidly because of human industrial and agricultural activity. This includes the burning of **fossil fuels** such as coal, gas and oil and the destruction of the equatorial rainforests.

If no action is taken soon to reduce the effects of global warming, temperatures could rise by 1.5°C (2.7°F) over the next sixty years. Areas of the world that are now very productive could become deserts, leading to drought and **famine** on a massive scale. Sea-levels could rise by up to 50 cm by the year 2050, putting millions of people at risk from flooding in low-lying areas.

In the long term, the most important step towards reducing the threat of global warming is to cut the use of fossil fuels. We need to develop new ways of producing energy and make much better use of the energy we produce already.

Things to do – keeping a cloud diary

The various types of clouds you see in the sky are formed by different conditions in the atmosphere. From only three main cloud types – stratus, cumulus and cirrus, ten cloud formations can be identified. The study of clouds can tell us a great deal about the coming weather.

Watch the speed of clouds as they travel across the sky. If they move leisurely, present fine weather should continue. When clouds begin to scud rapidly across the sky, look out for wind and rain.

Height is also important. Clouds may form high in the sky at the end of a fine spell. This means the change from fine to rainy weather will be gradual, but the poorer weather may last some time.

If small clouds of the late afternoon melt away towards sunset, fine weather is likely. If cloud increases to cover the sky, expect unsettled weather the following day. During the daytime, if the clouds have

Cumulus and cirrus clouds can be seen on this fine summer day.

delicate edges merging softly into the blue background of the sky, this is a sign of fine weather. If they have edges that stand out against the sky, stormy weather is approaching.

The last thing to look for is direction. See if the higher clouds are moving in a

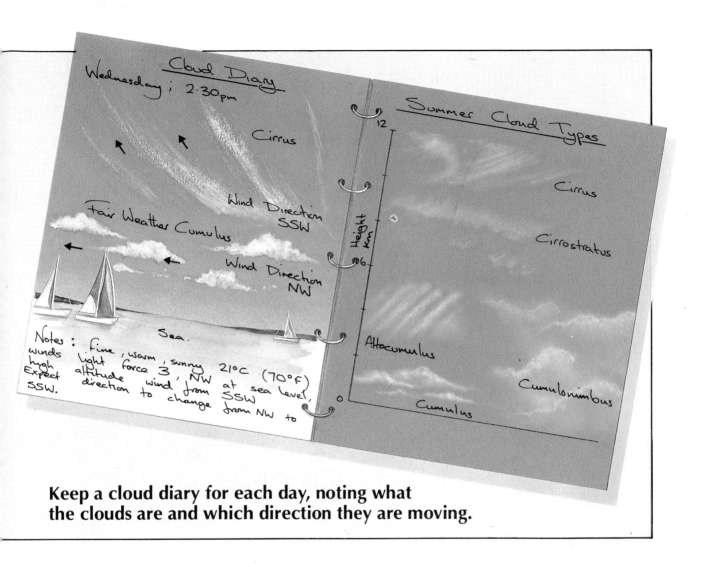

Keep a cloud diary for each day, noting what the clouds are and which direction they are moving.

different direction to the wind below or to lower layers of cloud. If they are, it means that the direction of the wind is about to change, and become the same direction as the higher clouds.

Keep a notebook and write down any changes you see in the clouds in one day. You could sketch some of the most interesting cloud formations. The next day you can enter details of the day's weather. This gives a good check on the accuracy of your cloud observations for forecasting weather.

GLOSSARY

Air pressure The force of layers of air in the atmosphere on the layers below, and on the ground.

Altitude Height above sea-level.

Antarctic The very cold land mass at the South Pole.

Arctic The cold lands and seas around the North Pole.

Axis An imaginary north-south line about which the Earth spins once every day.

Carbon dioxide A gas found in air formed from carbon and oxygen.

Charge A supply of positive or negative electrical energy.

Condense To turn water vapour into drops of liquid water by cooling.

Cumulus Cauliflower-shaped fluffy cloud which often appears in summer skies.

Dewpoint The temperature at which water vapour in the air starts to condense into water droplets.

Drought A long period of dry weather when no rain falls.

Equator A line completely encircling the Earth midway between the North and South Poles.

Equatorial Trough A band of low-pressure air along the Equator.

Famine An extreme shortage of food in an area leading to hunger and starvation.

Fossil fuel Fuel such as coal, oil and natural gas, made from the remains of living matter.

Front The boundary between a mass of cold and a mass of warm air.

Hailstones Pellets of ice which form in clouds and may fall to the ground.

Hemisphere Half of the Earth's sphere.

Latitude A measure of how far north or south of the Equator a place on the Earth's surface lies.

Poles The extreme north and south of the Earth.

Saturated When air will not absorb any more water vapour at a given temperature.

Spark A discharge of electricity, accompanied by a flash of light.

Supercell A long-lived and particularly violent thunderstorm within which tornadoes may form.

Temperate regions The areas having a moderate, mild climate between the tropics and the polar regions.

Tornado A devastating funnel-shaped whirlwind which extends to the ground and sucks up objects in its path.

Tropics The very warm areas on the Earth's surface which stretch across the Equator.

Tundra The treeless semi-frozen plains of northern Arctic regions.

Waterspout A column of water and mist caused by a whirlwind passing over water.

BOOKS TO READ

Bramwell, Martyn, **Weather** (Franklin Watts, 1987)
Gribbin, John, and Gribbin, Mary, **Weather** (Macdonald, 1985)
Lambert, David, and Hardy, Ralph, **Weather and its Work** (Orbis, 1988)
McInnes, Celia, **Projects for Summer** (Wayland, 1989)
Rosen, Mike, **Summer Festivals** (Wayland, 1990)
Whitlock, Ralph, **Summer** (Wayland, 1986)

PICTURE ACKNOWLEDGEMENTS

The publishers would like to thank the following for allowing their pictures to be reproduced in this book: Bryan & Cherry Alexander 5 (right); Bruce Coleman Ltd cover, 8 (Dr Eckart Pott), 14 (Dieter and Mary Plage), 15 (D. Houston), 18 (W. Carlson/Lane), 25 (Leonard Lee Rue), 27 (Dieter and Mary Plage); Frank Lane Picture Agency Ltd 13, 19 (both), 20, 22 (both); the Hutchison Library 21 (top), 23, 24 (top); J.Allen Cash Ltd 12; the Meterological Office (R.K Pilsbury) 28; Tony Stone Worldwide inside cover, 7, 16, 21 (bottom), 24 (bottom); Wayland Picture Library 4 (Chris Fairclough), 26; Zefa 5 (left), 6. All artwork by the Hayward Art Group, except page 6 by Peter Bull Art.

INDEX

Numbers in **bold** refer to illustrations